BLAZERS

MILITARY VEHICLES

# U.S.
# MARINE CORPS
# ASSAULT VEHICLES

by Angie Peterson Kaelberer

**Reading Consultant:**
Barbara J. Fox
Reading Specialist
North Carolina State University

Capstone
press

Mankato, Minnesota

Blazers is published by Capstone Press,
151 Good Counsel Drive, P.O. Box 669, Mankato, Minnesota 56002.
www.capstonepress.com

*Library of Congress Cataloging-in-Publication Data*
Kaelberer, Angie Peterson.
　　U.S. Marine Corps assault vehicles / by Angie Peterson Kaelberer.
　　p. cm.—(Blazers. Military vehicles)
　　Summary: "Describes amphibious assault vehicles, or AAVs, their design,
equipment, weapons, crew, missions, and role in the U.S. Marine Corps"—
Provided by publisher.
　　Includes bibliographical references and index.
　　ISBN-13: 978-0-7368-6456-5 (hardcover)
　　ISBN-10: 0-7368-6456-3 (hardcover)
　　1. Amphibious assault ships—United States—Juvenile literature. 2. United
States. Marine Corps—Juvenile literature. I. Title. II. Series.
V895.K34 2007
623.7'475—dc22　　　　　　　　　　　　　　　　　　　2006002794

**Editorial Credits**
Martha E. H. Rustad, editor; Thomas Emery, set designer; Ted Williams, book
　　designer; Jo Miller, photo researcher/photo editor

**Photo Credits**
AP/Wide World Photos/Itsuo Inouye, 21 (bottom)
Check Six 2005/Sam Sargent, 13 (bottom), 24–25; Ted Carlson, 14; Tom
　　Twomey, 22–23
Corbis/Reuters/Oleg Popov, 19
DVIC/CWO3 Seth Rossman, USNR, 13 (top)
Getty Images Inc./Joe Raedle, 6–7; USMC/Sgt. Joseph R. Chenelly, 21 (top)
Photo by Ted Carlson/Fotodynamics, 4–5, 28–29
U.S. Navy Photo by JO2 (SW) Brian P. Biller, 10, 26; JO2 Zack Baddorf,
　　16–17; PH1 Brien Aho, 8–9; PH2 Prince A. Hughes III, cover, 18; PHAA
　　Erik K. Siegel, 27; PHAN Sarah E. Ard, 11

**Capstone Press thanks Herb Muktarian, Director of Communications for
BAE Systems, Ground Systems Division, York, Pennsylvania, for his
assistance in preparing this book.**

1 2 3 4 5 6 11 10 09 08 07 06

# TABLE OF CONTENTS

# ASSAULT VEHICLES

A vehicle cuts through the ocean waves. It quickly reaches the shore. Then, it drives up on the beach. No boat can do that! The vehicle is an assault amphibious vehicle, or AAV.

The U.S. Marine Corps uses AAVs to carry Marines to mission sites on water and land. The current model is the AAV7A1.

## BLAZER FACT

The AAV7A1 carries up to 21 Marines.

# DESIGN

The AAV moves smoothly through water and over land. Two water jet pumps push it through water. A set of wheels and tracks roll the AAV over ground.

TRACK

WHEEL

AAVs move through rivers, lakes, and oceans. Even 10-foot (3-meter) waves can't slow them down.

# BLAZER FACT

The AAV7A1 has a top speed of 45 miles (72 kilometers) per hour on land and 8 miles (13 kilometers) per hour in water.

AAVs don't need roads. Their tracks glide over desert sand, muddy swamps, and rocky hills.

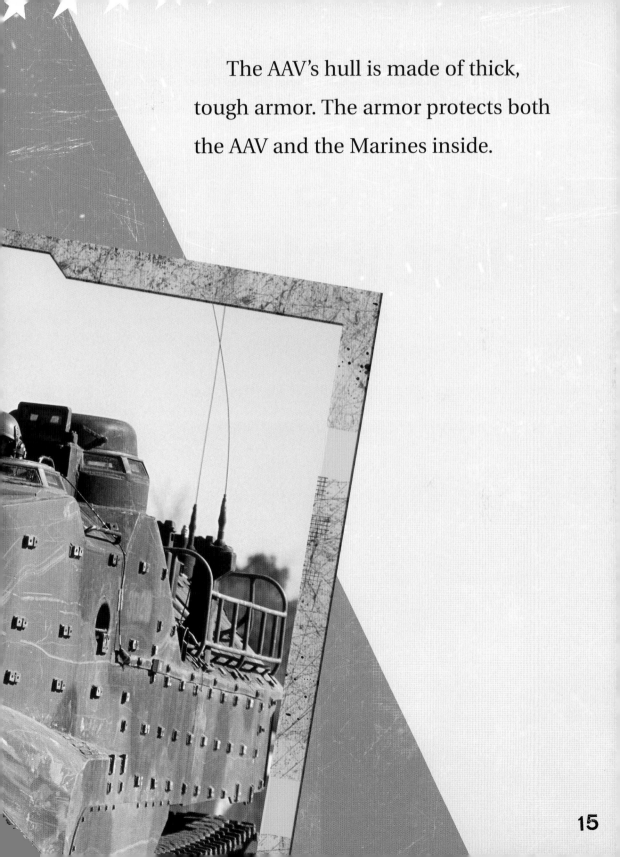

The AAV's hull is made of thick, tough armor. The armor protects both the AAV and the Marines inside.

# WEAPONS AND EQUIPMENT

An AAV's main use is moving Marines and gear from ship to shore. Once on land, it takes Marines where they are needed. An AAV carries weapons, but only to defend itself.

An MK-19 grenade launcher is attached to the AAV's turret. The launcher can hurl grenades at targets nearly 1 mile (1.5 kilometers) away.

AAVR-7

MK-19

# BLAZER FACT

Marines use the AAVR-7 to fix and help other vehicles. It is lightly armed with an M-60 machine gun.

AAVs have an M-2 machine gun. The gun fires up to 550 bullets each minute.

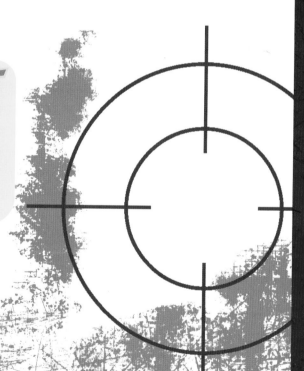

## BLAZER FACT

AAVs can carry up to 10,000 pounds (4,500 kilograms) of cargo.

.50-CALIBER M-2

# AAV DIAGRAM

TURRET

HULL

TRACK

HATCH

WHEEL

# THE CREW AND ITS MISSION

A driver, gunner, and vehicle commander make up the AAV crew. They drive the vehicle and fire the weapons.

WELL DECK

When a mission is over, the AAV travels back to its home aboard a Navy ship. The driver guides it into a well deck. It will stay there until the next mission.

# READY FOR ACTION!

# GLOSSARY

**amphibious** (am-FIB-ee-uhss)—able to work on land or water

**grenade** (gruh-NAYD)—a small explosive device that often is thrown at enemy targets

**hull** (HULL)—the frame or body of a vehicle that supports the other vehicle parts

**launcher** (LAWN-chur)—a tool that fires grenades

**mission** (MISH-uhn)—a military task

**turret** (TUR-it)—a rotating structure on top of a military vehicle that holds a weapon

**well deck** (WEL DEK)—an area on the lower level of a ship that can be flooded to hold water vehicles

# READ MORE

**Doeden, Matt.** *U.S. Marine Corps.* U.S. Armed Forces. Mankato, Minn.: Capstone Press, 2005.

**Hamilton, John.** *The Marine Corps.* Defending the Nation. Edina, Minn.: Abdo, 2006.

**Stone, Lynn M.** *Amphibious Assault Ships.* Fighting Forces on the Sea. Vero Beach, Fla.: Rourke, 2006.

# INTERNET SITES

FactHound offers a safe, fun way to find Internet sites related to this book. All of the sites on FactHound have been researched by our staff.

Here's how:
1. Visit *www.facthound.com*
2. Choose your grade level.
3. Type in this book ID **0736864563** for age-appropriate sites. You may also browse subjects by clicking on letters, or by clicking on pictures and words.
4. Click on the **Fetch It** button.

**FactHound will fetch the best sites for you!**

# INDEX